The Musing Muse

Supriya Arora

BookLeaf Publishing

India | USA | UK

Presentation by *BookLeaf Publishing*

Web: www.bookleafpub.com

E-mail: info@bookleafpub.com

ISBN: 9789358315677

First edition 2023

DEDICATION

Dedicated to my loved ones

ACKNOWLEDGEMENT

Heartfelt thanks to my family and friends for unwavering support and encouragement throughout this journey. Your love and understanding have been my constant inspiration. I would like to acknowledge the dedicated team at BookLeaf Publishing for providing wonderful opportunities. Your tireless efforts have transformed my manuscript into a published work of art. Your commitment to the written word is truly commendable.

PREFACE

In this enchanting journey through the corridors of my heart, these poems are the keys that unlock the doors to a world where emotions dance in vivid colors and words paint the canvas of the soul. You will be on a roller coaster of emotional depth and sensitivity.
You will find the beauty to embrace love, grief and the resilience of the human spirit. Each poem is a carefully woven tapestry of emotions, a reflection of my soul, and also an invitation for you to explore your own.
Allow them to wash over you, to inspire, to heal you and to remind you that the emotions we share as humans connect us in a montage of our existence.

Hope you enjoy reading the book as much as I loved writing it.

Guru Gobind Singh Ji

When you and the ONE
Are in the same zone
You discover not only your eyes and cheeks
But your clothes are wet with those
Divine tears
Then you go through the flashback
What made it happen.

In eyes closed
Drops a dream, and
A bright light
And there you find your guru
When you are chasing Him
with joy and bliss
He on His horse is;
laughing and smiling
Because the inner child in you is
As innocent as a lamb
But brave as a lion
(For He made his generations
The bravest of all:
Brave in mind and manner
In action and thought).
Fervently jumping, running and galloping
Like the horse to follow him

Until He suddenly halts,
And climbs down the horse
Take His stance in a position of rest
In the most majestic and gigantic form.
And you
So superhumanly amazed by this magnetism of
His
Lie down stomach flat on the ground
With your hands clasped on top of your head
For you cannot bear this irresistible charm and
charisma slowly and gradually
He shows his mercy and blesses you
By absorbing you in himself
Where there is no you
But
Only HIM
It's cold in there but
Most lovingly warm in heart
Where you cannot utter a single syllable
And the tsunami of tears has been tantalized
And this ocean of tears
Has swept away all the fears
As if they never were there.
Blessed, just blessed
Nothing more to say.

Wish

For I have loved
From the depths of my heart,
Fulfilled every promise
That I ever vowed.
No stones left unturned
I wish and believe
Even after death,
I would be loved
Like the way everyone loves me now,
And be remembered in the way that
I would still twinkle with a smile
In their hearts and eyes
In the tears, if ever they would roll.

Dear Mind

How do I like
The task that I do
Dear heart, answered the mind,
Do the needful
And no question would arise
It will be just beautiful through.

The Positive One

Who do I need right now???
Someone or no one?
I am the whole,
The positive one
Who stood by my own side?
I am the river,
Always Forgiving and moving on
Then I see myself like the valley
The Valley of self and love
Where I peacefully restore
Like the calm sky and the calm waters below
Only pals had a standby
In light and in rain
In thunder and in pain
And also those who were my bearers
And of course those for who I cared.
To all of them
I extend from the core
The loveliest of flowers
That my heart could hold.

Little Birdie

They gave the bird a big home
But the birdie called it a cage,
With Gold and pearls and diamonds
Though; that home was beautifully
staged.
They would jewel the house for bird
But they never let it loose
For they feared the little one's freedom
As if in hawk it could grow.
Little did they know
It only wanted to touch the sky
Gliding with the wind; up and down
Luxuriate the blue, never have a frown;
As if it was a dance in the air
It wanted to tweet the songs here-
Sometimes gently,
Sometimes; just in notes high.
But now in the cage, it only cries.
Big tears, that water of salinity
Drowned the birdie's joy,
day and night.
'Let me fly, I promise to return,
And dance for you every time.'
But not a soul could hear
The sound of despair, hence;

Screams became sobs
and sobs to sighs,
Sighs turned dispiriting
as the bird now construed
In that cage
It was destined to die.

Capture Moments

They say
Why do we need pictures everyday
When every page of life would be turned over
When the mirror would show us
The greys in head down the shoulder
These pictures will show us what we would
want to see
The glorious past
The show of spectacle
The era of beauty and youth
Which would have been faded by that time these
pictures when we will see
And will recall the times
Spent best with our loved ones.

Quarantined

I hear the mommies saying
To their little heartthrobs
'Get up my child
It's already past 8 o'clock.'
I look at my kids and see
It's way more than we should care.

They tell me that the sun rises everyday
And sets in a discipline
And that the moon takes the throne
When the sun has already shone.
It's the early bird that catches the worm.
That those who follow the drill of
Early to bed and early to rise
Makes them really healthy, wealthy and wise.

So go my child, sleep well, get up well
For the next day you are going to drain
So what if it's quarantine
A routine to follow is of reason prime
That a set pattern makes them hearty and hale
Never mind the school is off
And surely they are off routine
For the usual busy little bee.

To them I say
Yes, the sun
Even the sun doesn't rise
The same minute everyday
So doesn't the moon,
It too, waxes and wanes
Every season, Every day
And those seasons,
Even they are not the same.
The brightest star fades sometimes
And it's all good in this game.

Let's not make the task tedious
For a lifetime they have been ahead
Let's just discipline softly
For the world would be hard
Let them have a sleep
Full of dreams,
Which they would toil to achieve.
Let's leave them aside
As for a while
After the break as they emerge
Young soldiers and Knights.

Prayer

When I sit for my prayers
I find myself
In my master's palace
Guilded with gold
Spreading its solace
To young and old.
Looks like quite an early morning
When from the sun
There's nothing that you can hear.

I bow myself
Not only my head and neck,
But I lay as a whole;
Hands clasped
All I do is, just bow down, Him, before.
The soul is obsequious as well
Not just my body though.
He blessed me with His merciful words
More sweet than anything sweeter in this world.
I take a dip in the holy pond
To wash away my fears
And pray to Him again
To keep me always near.
It's a reverie, I know
But I believe
My soul and I, are in, Golden Temple though.

Wordsworth

Oh Wordsworth
To you I owe,
an ode
For sharing the words of your heart
To mine.
To the Wye River, I wish we walked together,
And saw those dancing daffodils and maybe,
Some other day;
Be in their happy company.
Since then, until today
To the highland yet another stroll,
And a glimpse of the reaper we catch together
And from you directly I would hear
Her songs of melancholy.
Up and down the hills, I wish!
Playfully we roll
Like a roe or fawn,
Or chase that cloud flying frantically
Up in the sky blue.
A wish to see your world
With your eyes and words
But with you, directly in front of me.
And I:
reciprocate it with all the love
My heart can hold forever.

Lonely In The Crowd

No one to talk to
No heart to beat with,
Here I sit,
Sit All alone.

Amidst the crowd
No smile, no frown
Not a soul knows me,
I wish to hear a sound.
Sound of fun
Sound of a heartbeat
Some sound that
Stirs the persona up in air
I don't want to sound
Like the child of melancholy
But be a person whose heart
Is full of ecstasy.

Friends!!!

When one has a heart full of love
Tethered and bound only with love
The joy and peace from only love
Same thought process
And it's just love.

No insults felt
No egos hurt
No one knows what
Is to be controlled.
Where your sorrows are theirs
And their joys are yours;
Those blissful laughs
The smile in the eyes,
You can see,
And of course
those tears from eyes;
Yes, those tears from eyes,
Only drop,
When you know
No fun is made
And you know it's your mistake,
Or maybe
Just on seeing that shoulder
That you know,

you can always lean on
And cry as long
Till eternity goes on...
When you are made happy
Only by reminding a song,
Or just by mimicking
Your stupidest self
But they know
This is how
They put a smile on your face.
Even miles apart
They know
If you are happy or sad
Feeling low or just ecstatic
Or won a medal or lost a game
Or you just want a picture
Together in frame.
Feel blessed
Even if you have only one
with all these merits
Just conjugate
For they are the ones
Hard to find
In this treacherous and heinous world
Where pulling someone down is not a crime.
So stay with them,
With your real friends,
Know their worth
See how much they care

As not only from mines, but,
all kinds of diamonds are your best friends.

Vacant Heart and Palms

The neck drooped
In deep distress
And the hands clasped the face tight
Palms found wet.
Eyes swollen, throat choked
And a wrenched heart, a heavy heart
A depressed heart, a melancholic heart
A heart full of affliction.
How does one carry this,
And leave;
For everything is broken
To the millionth bit inside.

It's brittle and it shatters, well
with such ease,
Even upon knowing that
this is how they, every time; retreat.
But alas!!!
It's been battered for times incomputable,
No fixations left
No glue can plaster it any more.
Yet; when it's a sunny day
It smiles again, as if it doesn't know
The occurrence of the shady ceremony
on the grey, gloomy day before.

In this hammering and mending process
Of making up the mind,
I struggle to see
What lies beneath,
Under the abundant desolate bleakly show.
The blood travels through the body daily
To keep the flame in the frame go.
But no one knows
That it is just the carcass
Only carcass,
Unmistakably, not the soul.
It beats and pumps the vital fluids
But
In spirit, just void hands it shows.

These vacant palms do not know
What next they have to hold.
The new greed is happiness
For all the smiles are lost to grief,
Leaving a sulk, to trail behind;
A weakened body, mind and soul.
Not much worth than an organ works
The heart Has turned into a lump.
It beats for others,
But for itself, it nothing broods.
Left with such a lifeless life
I wonder again
How quickly and instantly it recapitulates
To resume its course in the rut of life

Stipulating for a normal self
With or without a mask.

Nature- My Guiding Spirit

I looked for you in the Swiss Alps
And in the German forest too.
In the French terrain,
You were the same
Deep shade in Ypres you drew.
I wish I could see you in the English
countryside,
Just like in the Rockies I visit you.
But a new awakening dawns on me
Nature
It's you that I really love
Not just a places few.
Like one god,
The Almighty one,
Omnipotent and omnipresent; you're
Just one force with many names
And I found you at every inch
Wherever my eyes extended to.
Soft whispers in my ears I hear
That it's with you that I want myself
Forever, never ask for an adieu.

Be my guiding spirit and a healer
For I yearn to be enveloped in your arms
Like the most revered Wordsworth said

'Nature never did betray the heart that loved her'
So I will love you like my own god,
Like my own parents I would do;
For you teach marvellous lessons
In spring, summer, fall and winter
Like my pro creator always drew,
Bloom in every field and shine,
Ripe when the time is right,
Part but with good colours,
But cold to those who turn cold,
Yet keep your cozy sides besides.

Further more you force me
To just agree, and nothing less
Even if the seasons change,
United you stand
From the sky, the cloud and the earth below
To the extended universe too,
Bedazzled with the best
Like the finest lady would always prove.
So I surrender myself
To the greatest master
To learn, enjoy and meditate
And breathe deeply in your vicinity
Until it's time to proceed
For the destination next
And sublime in you completely.

Solitary But Gallant

Alone
But strong
Alas!!!
Not lonely at least
The head held high
The Crown..
Nah, just the coronet,
The invisible coronet,
Right in its place!!!
The powerful silence
That speaks words, phrases
And clauses
By just configuring the stillness
Celebrating tranquility
Of the solitary being
In the state of unadulterated solo self
For the mind and heart;
After the cruelties of life;
Amalgamated into one....
Who carefully and cautiously
Took heed in being a friend
In all honesty, a confidante...
But with no surprises
The world doesn't care
What the empaths and the cherished

Feel...
But this strong heart and mind
Heads with a stronger soul
Leaves the frailties in all forms
And pursues its own path
Of being alone
Yet a new incarnation of the old entity
New and Happy♥

On the way to Bath

On the road called M4
Off we go to see the most loved resident
Of Bath, it's Jane Austen, should I reveal?
Crossing and traversing trucks and cars; woods
and trees
Feasting my eyes on rolling hills and sandwalls;
horses and sheep,
Chugging the beauty of the area of outstanding
natural beauty,
It occurs in my mind why would everyone not
become Shakespeare, Wordsworth or Coleridge.
What a sheer bolt of luck in my life that I have
To witness, visit and preserve this gift for
eternity.
Could there be anything more filled with
romance
To feel the Romantics in their demesne.

Time and Age

At what stage I am now
Is second adolescence
Not a kid not an adult
You don't know where you are.
But there's a difference of hope.
Then, the vigor was full,
Was a desire to conquer the world.
But now, it's an energy drain
Where then a happening life was wanted,
A calm and serene existence is looked for.
It's just time and space
Let's see what comes with age.

Rise like a Phoenix

Just like the Phoenix
O my hollowed spirit
Rise, rise and rise...
Rise again from your ashes
From your mind, you get the power
And your heart brings thee wings
Thy soul propels the morales up
And again you erect like a king
Show the world thy worthy self
And raise the chalice up high
Let them know you will grow again
Out of agony, out of pain
No matter how they put you down
Show the courage; come, put that gown
Of valour not audacity; yet
Hiding that gentle side
For the soft corners
They think you need
So return their fears, with pride,
Proud of being your able self
And where egos never flied
Let them know your capacities
Reaching far and wide
And with a dash of graciousness
Emerge in the beautiful new daylight.

So rise and emerge again
Just like the Phoenix.

Mind and the Heart

Why does everyone trample me
Under careless tread, with his feet,
Slowly said the heart
In his faintest beat.
Anticipation at its best you keep
From those who do nothing
To make you please
Said the thoughtful mind
In a simple voice fine.

Quietest Moments

Just when the moments were the quietest
Then were the feelings the loudest,
The cracking of the dreams
And an arrow that punctured the red mass
Was never seen
But to the heart, the damage was great
Like the volcano
Gargling lava
And vomiting red hot ambers
Which even if one wants can never be held
With hands.
Like saving the self from the fire
Burns the hands
Even though everything, just
Seems to be in its own place.

Spring

Let's watch and learn, from those trees
whose 'flags of summer' are ready for a rebirth;
to rejuvenate and reincarnate, enjoy a
renaissance after bravely withstanding the
atrocities of harsh cold winds and chills of the
grave winter.
Perfect snag for the tree to forget the
impediments, to forget what they lost to fall and
frost.
It's time to burst the lull and gloom,
To give life another chance and bloom,
Replenish all its vacancies again.
Not generally do we encounter, second chances
in life, But when nature volunteers, never should
we miss like these trees in spring.
Do not mull over to lose over and over again; let
the Spring, spring, new opportunities like the
Phoenix from its ashes; let's re-emerge.